God Bless

Transformed
by LOVE

Liz Babbs (signature)

Liz Babbs

Transformed
by LOVE

PRAYERS
AND
REFLECTIONS
FOR ALL
SEASONS

CWR

This book is dedicated to all those who have journeyed
with me as a writer across the last fifteen years. Thank you
for cheering me on! I never know when inspiration is going
to strike, but all my books undergo a significant journey.
This one is no exception and although written in Britain
across many years, the title emerged during a road trip from
Oregon to California. I'm grateful to Kim Bagato who helped
me organise these prayers at a point when I couldn't see the
wood for the trees – or the redwoods for the sequoias!

Transformed by Love is also available as a CD from Liz Babbs'
website **www.lizbabbs.com**

Contents

Introduction

Three things will last forever—faith, hope, and love—and the greatest of these is love.
1 Corinthians 13:13, NLT

Everyone goes through different seasons in life. Sometimes things go well and life is good, while at other times, everything seems to go wrong and you're left wondering whether anything will return to 'normal'. *Transformed by Love* is a collection of personal prayers and reflections written across the last fifteen years during various seasons of my life.

No matter what season we go through, God is always there for us. His transforming love and faithfulness shines through every aspect of our lives. Like the well-known 'Footprints' poem, I can see His loving imprints everywhere. As Scripture reminds us, we are one body with many parts (1 Corinthians 12:12), and there have been countless occasions when I've been carried through difficult situations by the love and prayers of others. I've come to realise that God is completely trustworthy – He will complete what He has started (1 Thessalonians 5:24 and Philippians 1:6).

Prayer, like poetry, is the language of love. When I write, I'm writing from the intensity of my feelings and so am often unaware whether I'm writing poetry or prayers. I'm in good company as the psalmists expressed their emotions in poetic form, creating some of the most beautiful and evocative prayers ever written. While some psalms express praise and worship, others are desperate cries for help and reveal the rawness of the human condition. But love always triumphs – everything is transformed by God's love.

My prayer, in writing *Transformed by Love*, is that it will help you deepen your understanding of God's unconditional love, and, if you're struggling to connect with God, will provide a bridge for you to walk across to Him.

Liz Babbs

ONE

Transformation of Love

I have loved you, my people, with an everlasting love. With unfailing love I have drawn you to myself.
Jeremiah 31:3, NLT

The origin of all love is God (1 John 4:7–8). We were made from love – for love. Love transforms us; we expand and grow in response to its life-changing power. And the love we express to others is a reflection of God's love for us.

Love Reigns

Let love *live*
In our hearts and minds.
Let love *rule*
Over our hopes and fears.
Let love *reign*
In our families and friendships.

Healing Love

Lord, Your love supports
strengthens
enfolds.
Binds up the brokenhearted.
Touches the point of pain.
Gives grace to forgive.

Love's Flow

Lord, Your love
pours itself out for me
Accepts me as I am
Heals my brokenness,
and flows through me to others.

Love of God

Love of God
Enfold me.
Spirit of God
Renew me.
Power of God
Infuse me.

God Loves

Passionately and unconditionally
God loves.
Completely and utterly
God loves.
Now and forever
God loves.

TWO

Journey of Love

*'What no eye has seen, what no ear has heard, and
what no human mind has conceived' – the things
God has prepared for those who love him*
1 Corinthians 2:9

In prayer, we learn how to be real before God as we
share our hopes and fears, anger and frustration,
our joys and disappointments. But prayer is also
about listening – listening to the voice of the One
who calls us, the loving shepherd who directs
our journey.

The Good Shepherd

You're the ground of my being
the reason for all hope.
The Good Shepherd
whose voice
leads me
into holy obedience.
The eternal Lover of the world
whose love draws me close
and closer still.

He makes me lie down in green pastures;
he leads me beside still waters
Psalm 23:2, NRSV

Streams of Water

I want clear streams of water
running through my head.

I want clear streams of water
not a mind that's half dead.

I want clear streams of water
to flush out the dregs.

I want clear streams of water
so my soul is refreshed.

Pilgrims

We are people of the way
searching for landmarks
for our heart's journey.

Listening –
to the voice of the Spirit.

Listening –
to the voice of the soul.

Journeying onwards
towards the pearl of great price.

For it is by grace you have been saved, through faith – and this is not from yourselves, it is the gift of God
Ephesians 2:8

Less is More

Love of God
Help me to be kind
To see the needs of the poor.
Spirit of God
Help me to be less
That I might see You more.

Homecoming

The landscape of our lives
bears the wounds of the One
who created us.
Seared through with love
we are beckoned homeward.

THREE
Image of Love

For we are God's masterpiece. He has created us anew in Christ Jesus, so we can do the good things he planned for us long ago.
Ephesians 2:10, NLT

God created us in His image as His masterpiece. Just as the potter shapes the clay, so our Master Potter moulds us into the image of His Son. Over time, God continues that process, chipping away at the raw material of our lives to reveal His divine beauty.

Master Creator

Master Creator:
When I write
I'm Your poem.
When I conduct
I'm Your symphony.
When I sculpt
I'm Your work of art.
And when I paint
I'm Your masterpiece.

Crafted from Love

Lord, Your faithfulness
cancels out my sense of worthlessness.
I am significant because You made me.
Crafted from love
I'm Your work of art.

Here's another way to put it: You're here to be light, bringing out the God-colors in the world. God is not a secret to be kept.

Matthew 5:14, *The Message*

The Author

Today is an empty page.
A wonderful space.
An open canvas
for me to fill
with a kaleidoscope
of colours and shades
of my choosing.
An endless palette
of possibilities.

For you created my inmost being; you knit me together in my mother's womb. I praise you because I am fearfully and wonderfully made

Psalm 139:13–14

Made in Love's Image

Thank You, Lord,
for the cutting and weaving,
for that first umbilical knot.
You were shaping
and forming
all that I was to become.

Thank You, Lord,
for the 'ups' and 'downs',
the 'unders' and the 'overs'.
You were weaving
beauty and purpose
into my life.

Sacred Tapestry

Lord, You have made
each person
a precious thread,
open ended with creative possibility
who when linked to others
weaves a community of beauty –
a sacred tapestry
mirroring heaven.

FOUR

Landscapes of Love

Sing to God a brand-new song.
He's made a world of wonders!
Psalm 98:1, *The Message*

Creation is God's work of art – a beautiful expression
of His love for us. Many of the psalms remind us that
God reveals Himself to us through creation.

Creation Presence

The calm of a summer night
embodies Your peace, O Lord.

The beauty of a sunset
embodies Your truth, O Lord.

The glory of the dawn
embodies Your faithfulness, O Lord.

Everything in all creation
shouts the reality of You.

You will keep in perfect peace all who trust in you,
all whose thoughts are fixed on you!
Isaiah 26:3, NLT

Finding Peace

Standing
alone on a beach
I am stirred
by the breath
of an infinite God
whose eyes search
the depths of my soul
and I am strangely
at peace.

Island Praise

Lord, make me an island
set apart for You
Where the rock of ages
rings out with praise
The waters of Your Spirit
saturate my soul
And the fire of Your presence
burns deep within.

Waterscape

Water
  stills my soul
    calms my mind
        and brings peace to
            my
                inner
                    being.

Deep calls to deep in the roar of your waterfalls;
all your waves and breakers have swept over me.
Psalm 42:7

Soaked in Your Love

Lord, I long for streams of living water
to burst forth with fountains of joy.
I want to be soaked –
soaked in the river
of Your love.

Love that Moulds History

Lord, Your love is the life force
shaping all creation.
The very essence we breathe.
Your love removes boundaries
eradicates prejudice
crosses divides
builds community
and moulds
history.

FIVE
Locations of Love

*Stand at the crossroads and look; ask for the
ancient paths, ask where the good way is, and walk
in it, and you will find rest for your souls.*
Jeremiah 6:16

When I travel across Britain I am sometimes so
arrested by the presence of God in a place, I have
to write! These poetic reflections were inspired by a
variety of locations I've visited by land and sea.

Iona

A place to lose myself
A place to find myself
A place of journey's end
A place of journey's beginning

Lindisfarne

On Lindisfarne
walking in the footsteps
of Saint Cuthbert
I know I am standing
on holy ground.
Sacred steps that prayed,
surrendered,
sacrificed,
saved.
And their memory lingers on ...
An inspirational presence
saturating the landscape
with the holiness
of the One
true
God.

Rydal Mount

What idyllic peace I find in Wordsworth's garden.
A sanctuary between heaven and earth
where to pray flows as naturally as breathing.

Even towering trees express themselves here
and rise above the summer house
seemingly laden with ancient words.

And nature, imbued with Your presence,
wraps loving arms around me
and I'm held secure.

Curbar Edge

These granite rocks
are my cathedral,
my monastery.
Their sheer faces
jut out into the valley below
directing my path.
A refuge for the traveller
a haven for birds.
Time-weathered stones
to rest and to nest,
with so many
ancient stories to tell.

Chichester Cathedral

Angel voices ring out around these
ancient cloistered passageways
embodying creation's praise.
And harmonised prayer
borne on Spirit wings
rises heavenwards
as incense to a
most holy
God.

SIX

Restfulness of Love

Come with me by yourselves to a quiet place and get some rest.
Mark 6:31

Jesus often withdrew to a mountain or crossed
the lake so He could retreat from the crowds to
spend quality time with His Father. We also need to
withdraw from the busyness of life so we can rest
and be recharged. Psalm 23 reminds us that
we have all we need in God.

The LORD is my shepherd, I lack nothing.
Psalm 23:1

Shepherd Guidance

Lord, thank You that You are my shepherd
That You lead me and guide me.
Even when I'm far away from You
You look after me, supplying all my needs.

You give me strength when I feel like giving up
and make mountains into level paths for me.
You lead me beside still waters
and provide rest and refreshment
for my whole being.

Called by the Silence

I am called by the silence.
I am drawn by the silence.
As a lover calls his beloved into intimate embrace.
I am found in You.
My soul longs for You.
And that longing is consummated in silence
when we two become one.

Heaven's Wings

I am stirred by the breath of the infinite God,
who whispers
through desert sands,
hovers
over shimmering waters,
and rises
on heaven's wings.

Be Still and Know …

(Based on Psalm 46:10)

Be still and know that I am God
Be still and know that I AM
Be still and KNOW
BE STILL
BE

Silence is …

A space to retreat.
A place to grow,
to be watered and fed.
To learn only those things
that flourish
in its soil.

A Quiet Place

There is a space within all of us,
a quiet place reserved for God.
Here, we can listen to His voice,
receive His love
and bask in His presence.
Go to that place now
and rest
relax,
and enjoy.

The Still Point

Lord,
In the storms of life
may I be still.

In the noise of life
may I find peace.

In the busyness of life
may I find rest.

And my God will meet all your needs according to the riches of his glory in Christ Jesus.
Philippians 4:19

Home in You

When my mind, body and spirit
are reconnected with You, Lord,
I know
I've come
home.

Faith is ...

Silence filled with expectation.
Prayer pregnant with hope.
Trust in deepest darkness.
A light shining the way.

Faith is waiting and knowing,
allowing God to direct.
Faith is listening and growing
as He carefully orders each step.

Carry Me

Lord,
Carry me into Your presence
Enfold me into You
Raise me to the heavens
For I long to draw closer to You.

SEVEN

Balance of Love

Be well balanced (temperate, sober of mind),
be vigilant and cautious at all times; for that enemy
of yours, the devil, roams around like a lion roaring
[in fierce hunger], seeking someone
to seize upon and devour.

1 Peter 5:8, Amplified

The Bible speaks with great authority about the
importance of work-life balance and warns us to be
'well balanced' because excess in one area of our lives
can lead to problems in another (1 Peter 5:8). Time is
a gift from God, so we need to seek His guidance on
how to use it.

Who am I?

Lord, who am I in the workplace?
Am I just a cog grinding against a wheel
squeezed into the machinery of life
where work dominates
and my spirit is quenched?

I have come that they may have life,
and have it to the full.
John 10:10

God our Bridge

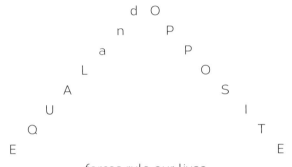

E Q U A L a n d O P P O S I T E
forces rule our lives.
We are drawn towards the truth
but tempted by evil.
We buckle under pressure
and snap when tension mounts.
But if You are our bridge, Lord,
stability is assured
because You are our load bearer
allowing us to walk free.

Finding Balance

Lord, I don't know who I am,
what I'm doing
or where I'm going anymore.
But I give myself to You
and pray that You can restore some
order and b
                 a
                   l
                      a
                          n
                             c
                                e
from this   c h a o s

My times are in your hands
Psalm 31:15

The Gift of Time

Thank You, Lord,
that each day is a gift
if we learn how to live in it.
Each moment is precious
when we know
it could be
our
last.

God's Time

Time,
we live upon its
k
  n
    i
      f
        e
       e
     d
   g
    e.
We don't own time.
Time moves
in relation to God.

God's the Driver!

Lord, You are driving the car
and I'm Your passenger.
We travel together at Your speed,
so I don't need to worry.
We even have time to stop
and enjoy the countryside!

Even though I'm very busy
Your way is one of efficiency.
So instead of worrying,
I'll sit back and enjoy the ride!

You'll show me how to live a more balanced life,
then I'll really know how to enjoy myself,
because I'll be trusting in You for everything.

Meanwhile, I'll sit back and relax, because
You're in the driving seat, not me!

> *My grace is sufficient for you, for my power is made perfect in weakness.*
>
> **2 Corinthians 12:9**

The Power of Weakness

Thank You, Lord,	H.
that	T
in	G
my	N
weakness	E
lies	R
my	T
greatest	S

EIGHT
Test of Love

We experience love to the degree we are willing
to surrender ourselves to it. Many of us have had
painful experiences of love, but pain is the risk
love takes. Pain can lead to bitterness and cause a
person to shrink from further encounters with love,
but forgiveness is the key to open the padlock to
this closed door.

Likewise, the tongue is a small part of the body, but it makes great boasts. Consider what a great forest is set on fire by a small spark.

James 3:5

Words Carry

Words carry ...
Shaped and formed in mind and mouth.
Launched like torpedoes,
explode on impact
leaving a trail of tear gas.
A stench which
permeates
penetrates
annihilates.
Words carry ...

Help us to Forgive

Lord of all life,
grant us forgiveness
for our judgmental thoughts
and wrong attitudes.
For the poverty of our actions
and the words
with which we
wound.

Forgive us, Lord

We hold each other's lives
in our hands.
What fragility and responsibility.
Earthen vessels formed
from loving hands
so easily crushed
by clumsy words and actions.
And only forgiveness
can reassemble the parts
according to the Maker's instructions.

Trust in the LORD with all your heart and lean not on your own understanding; in all your ways submit to him, and he will make your paths straight.

Proverbs 3:5–6

Trust

Trust is a hard one to call ...
It's like a caged bird
with a wide open door.
It's an uncertain step
from boat to shore.
It's the first flight of an eaglet
in free fall.
It requires of me
not part, but all.
Maybe that's why
trust is a hard one to call.

God's Faithfulness

No matter what ...
God is with us.
No matter what ...
God is there.
No matter what ...
God is beside us,
Meeting us in despair.

No matter what ...
God loves us.
No matter what ...
God cares.
No matter what
load we may carry
It's one God will always bear.

No matter what ...
Jesus died to save us.
No matter what ...
He now lives.
No matter what ...
God's Spirit leads us,
and by His stripes
we now live.

'For I know the plans I have for you,' declares the
Lord, 'plans to prosper you and not to harm you,
plans to give you hope and a future.'
Jeremiah 29:11

When Hope Fades

When hope fades
faith withers
love shrivels
heart slumps
hands clench
and mirrors reflect
an angry present.
Future's window
is closed forever.

For he will conceal me there when troubles come;
he will hide me in his sanctuary. He will place me
out of reach on a high rock.
Psalm 27:5, NLT

Hope in Darkness

Lord,
It's at the vortex of light and dark
pain and suffering
hopelessness
and despair
that I
find
Y
O
U

Contemporary Beatitudes

To those who are lost
And ache for truth,
God brings His comfort.

To those who cry out for justice
But have no proof,
God brings His comfort.

To those who struggle to
Make ends meet,
God brings His comfort.

To those who don't have
Enough to eat,
God brings His comfort.

To those who are marginalised
And have no self-worth,
God brings His comfort.

To those who are beaten
And pushed down in the dirt,
God brings His comfort.

To those who are shackled
Without and within,
God brings His comfort.

To those whose life
Nears its end,
God brings His comfort.

NINE

Spirit of Love

For we know how dearly God loves us,
because he has given us the Holy Spirit
to fill our hearts with his love.

Romans 5:5, NLT

The Trinity is a divine dance of love. God's love
flows to us through the gift of His Son, and the
Holy Spirit infuses our hearts with that love.

God's Provision

Father, Spirit, Son, You care for me.
Father, Spirit, Son, You protect me.
Father, Spirit, Son, You guide me.
Father, Spirit, Son, You love me.

Trinitarian Blessing

I bless the Three in One
and the One in Three
Father
Spirit
Son
Thank You
for
Loving
Me

Threefold Joy

Joy of the Creator Father.
Joy of the Redeeming Son.
Joy of the Sustaining Spirit.
Lord, I rejoice in the Three in One.

Light of the World

Light of the world infiltrate my darkness.
Light of the world restore my strength.
Light of the world illuminate my pathway.
And grant me Your peace
that I might find my way home to You.

I Belong to You

Encircling arms of the Creator Father
I belong to You.
All embracing love of Jesus the Son
I belong to You.
Empowering presence of the Holy Spirit
I belong to You.

Peace Prayer

May the peace of God encircle you.
May the peace of Christ enfold you.
May the peace of the Spirit encompass you
this day and forever more.

Spirit of God

Spirit of God around me
In the air I breathe.

Glory of God around me
Inspiring all I see.

Joy of God around me
In laughter and in mirth.

Majesty of God around me
In the fruitfulness of the earth.

Son of God around me
In the creatures of this land.

Love of God around me
Holding my future in His hands.

TEN

Dance of Love

They that sing as well as they that dance shall say,
All my fountains are in thee.
Psalm 87:7, ASV

Before I became a writer I trained for many years
as a dancer and dance was how I expressed my
passion for God creatively. Now it's my words that
dance across the page!

Life's Dance

The dance of life.
The circle of joy.
The intimacy of the Creator
both Father and Lord.

praise him with tambourine and dancing,
praise him with the strings and pipe
Psalm 150:4

The Dance of Joy

Lord of the dance
Open my eyes
to Your glory,
Release my heart
to dance.

Beloved

Lord, I find You
in that solitary place
where heaven and earth kiss
and love's dance begins.

Well Done!

I've waited a lifetime it seems,
to be fully accepted for who I am.
To walk in the freedom of being me
To shed the layers of uncertainty.

I've waited a lifetime it seems,
to have the confidence to dance
to paint rainbows with my words
and allow You to direct my path.

I've waited a lifetime it seems,
to fill the gaping void
the depth of which is unfathomable
the pain of which most don't see.

I've waited a lifetime it seems,
to hear words that would release me
free me, complete me:
'I'm proud of you.
'Well done, good and faithful servant.'

ELEVEN

Celebration of Love

*His love has the first and last word
in everything we do.*
2 Corinthians 5:14, *The Message*

We often use poetry and prayers to commemorate
key events like weddings, anniversaries and
funerals. In the Christian calendar, Christmas and
Easter are special celebrations and remind us of the
eternal nature of God's love for us. I've also had the
privilege of writing prayers for friends to celebrate
their wedding or anniversary.

Wedding Prayer
– The Gift of Love

(Inspired by 1 Corinthians 13:4–7)

Love is patient
And so we come together
Love is kind
Drawn by You
It does not envy
Into Your holy presence
It does not boast
United by our love
It is not proud
Bound by Your promises
It does not dishonour others
Healed by Your love
It is not self-seeking
Lord, we seek to serve only You

It is not easily angered

Establish Your patience in us

It keeps no record of wrongs

And Your forgiveness

Love does not delight in evil but rejoices with the truth

Reveal to our hearts Your wisdom and truth

It always protects

Enfold us in Your love

Always trusts

Encircle us in Your care

Always hopes

Lead us forever onwards

Always perseveres.

Wedding Anniversary Prayer
– Thank You

Lord, for the years we've been together
Thank You
For the way You've held us in Your arms
Thank You
For Your faithfulness and steadfast love
Thank You
For the countless blessings You've showered upon us
Thank You
For the preciousness of touching other people's lives
Thank You
For our union and oneness which is only complete
in You
Thank You
For the blessing of family and extended family
Thank You
For calming the storms and being with us in the
turbulence
Thank You
For the privilege of knowing You
Thank You
Lord, what a precious gift to be Your children
and to know we will always be together in You.

Easter Passion

Stone upon stone
upon river
upon stream
my Lover is calling
He is beckoning to me.
A love consummated on a cross
and sealed in a tomb
we rise to new life
Bride and Bridegroom.

Christmas is Here!

Kings travel from afar
Christmas is coming.
Guided by the brightest star
Christmas is coming.
Bringing gold, frankincense and myrrh
Christmas is coming.
To the Son of Man
born on earth.
Christmas is here!

Christmas Joy

Your Word made flesh
A new translation.
Born into time and space
A fresh revelation.
Walks the earth
in moving meditation.
Delivering
Healing
Releasing
from condemnation.

The Real Work of Christmas

When the final present has been opened
and the last mouth fed,
When weariness spreads like a blanket over all
mankind,
The real work of Christmas begins:
To seek the lost
To support the lonely
To feed the starving
To shelter the homeless
To console the broken
To love the unlovely
To
LOVE.

New Year

New Year,
new hope
fresh challenges.
A chance to leave behind
what was,
and adventure into
what will be ...

TWELVE

Destination of Love

I am the resurrection and the life. Anyone who believes in me will live, even after dying. Everyone who lives in me and believes in me will never ever die.
John 11:25–26, NLT

Christianity is a journey with a destination and so God's love for us is not only unconditional, but eternal. As that journey nears its end, we realise that death is a gateway to a new beginning, a fulfilment of our life here on earth. Beyond this border country, a whole new landscape opens up and we discover that this is where our real adventure begins.

For those who find me find life and receive favour from the LORD.
Proverbs 8:35

The Journey

We journey to be together
We journey to escape
We journey to grow up
We journey to experience
We journey to share
We journey to change things
We journey to be free
We journey to discover
We journey to find ourselves
We journey to come home
But until we find our home in You
Our journey is incomplete.

Sacred Bridges

We are the bridges between the old and the new.
Between what was and what will be.
Between this generation and the next.
Drawn forever onward
into a future embracing love and hope.
An eternal destiny heavenward.

Desert Life

In the wilderness
I am found by You.
In the desert
I am watered by You.
In death
I am brought to new life.

The Journey Beyond

We all lose as we walk through life,
but grief is a friend, not a foe,
a teacher of wisdom,
a creative experience
that draws us closer to God.

When all falls apart in despair and sadness,
in God we are sustained
because He has been there before us
and grieves with us.

Who is to measure the length of a life
except God?

But we are enriched through the lives of others
and carried on the wings of their prayers,
and our friends
sent like missionaries from the heart of God
speak words of comfort to our fears.

Together for Eternity

And so, Lord,
somewhere in the distance we meet
Is it eternity
or some future time
Is there a nowness about it
a separation
and beyond
an otherness
but
togetherness
walking hand in hand
across
the
sands
of
time

New Beginnings

THE END …
Or is it the beginning of a new journey
stretching out before me?
An uncharted sea
that no one has returned from
except the One
who leads.

And surely I am with you always,
to the very end of the age.
Matthew 28:20

OTHER

Liz Babbs

TITLES

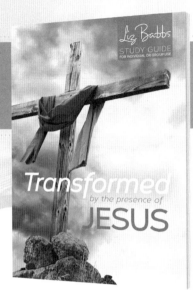

Transformed by the Presence of Jesus

Over six studies, Liz invites us to adopt a meditative
approach to reading Scripture. Go beyond traditional
Bible study and step into the shoes of many well-known
Bible characters, all of whom were transformed by their
encounters with Jesus.

Ideal for individual or group use.

ISBN: 978-1-78259-237-2

For current prices visit **www.cwr.org.uk/store**
Available online or from Christian bookshops

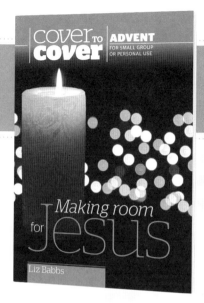

Making Room for Jesus
– Cover to Cover Advent Study Guide

In this Advent resource, Liz encourages us to make room for Jesus during, what can be for some, the busiest season of the year. Explore the themes of thanksgiving, obedience, surrender, intimacy, sacrifice and celebration over six studies.

Ideal for individual or group use.

ISBN: 978-1-78259-143-6

For current prices visit **www.cwr.org.uk/store**
Available online or from Christian bookshops

Continue transforming your daily walk with God.

Every Day with Jesus

With around half a million readers, this insightful devotional by Selwyn Hughes is one of the most popular daily Bible reading tools in the world. A large-print edition is also available.
72-page booklets, 120x170mm

Life Every Day

Apply the Bible to life each day with these challenging life-application notes written by international speaker and well-known author Jeff Lucas.
64-page booklets, 120x170mm

Inspiring Women Every Day

Written by women for women of all ages and from all walks of life. These notes will help to build faith and bring encouragement and inspiration to the lives and hearts of Christian women.
64-page booklets, 120x170mm

Cover to Cover Every Day

Study one Old Testament and one New Testament book in depth with each issue, and a psalm every weekend. Covers every book of the Bible in five years.
64-page booklets, 120x170mm

For current prices and to order visit www.cwr.org.uk/subscriptions
Also available online or from Christian bookshops

Seminars and events

Waverley Abbey College

Publishing and media

Conference facilities

Transforming lives

CWR's vision is to enable people to experience personal transformation through applying God's Word to their lives and relationships.

Our Bible-based training and resources help people around the world to:
• Grow in their walk with God
• Understand and apply Scripture to their lives
• Resource themselves and their church
• Develop pastoral care and counselling skills
• Train for leadership
• Strengthen relationships, marriage and family life, and much more.

Our insightful writers provide daily Bible reading notes and other resources for all ages, and our experienced course designers and presenters have gained an international reputation for excellence and effectiveness.

CWR's Training and Conference Centres in Surrey and East Sussex, England, provide excellent facilities in idyllic settings – ideal for both learning and spiritual refreshment.

Applying God's Word
to everyday life and relationships

CWR, Waverley Abbey House,
Waverley Lane, Farnham,
Surrey GU9 8EP, UK

Telephone: +44 (0)1252 784700
Email: info@cwr.org.uk
Website: www.cwr.org.uk

Registered Charity No. 294387
Company Registration No. 1990308